Words At Work
Vol. II

Carol L Rickard, LCSW

Well YOUniversity® Publications

www.WellYOUniversity.com

Copyright © 2013 Carol L Rickard

All Rights Reserved. No part of this book may be reproduced for resale, redistribution, or any other purposes (including but not limited to eBooks, pamphlets, articles, video, & handouts or slides for lectures or workshops) Permission to reproduce these materials for those and any other purposes must be obtained in writing from the author. Licensing is available for commercial use.

ISBN-13: 978-0-9821010-7-0

DEDICATION

This book is dedicated to all the patients I have had the privilege of working with..

CONTENTS

      Acknowledgments

1. Courage
2. Effort
3. Goals
4. Attitude
5. Faith
6. Urges
7. Feel
8. Give
9. Grow
10. Late
11. Love
12. Mistake
13. Music
14. Oprah
15. Practice
16. Priority
17. Save
18. Recovery
19. Serenity
20. Shame
21. Support
22. Today
23. Trust
24. What if
25. Whys
26. Fail
27. Reflect
28. Aware
29. Teachers
30. Nurses
31. Doctors
32. Lawyers
33. Team
34. Accept
35. Clarity
36. Action
37. Guilty
38. Respect
39. Bono
40. Joy
41. Grateful
42. Start
43. Creators
44. Dwell
45. Chaos
46. Food
47. Interpret
48. Trigger
49. Urges
50. Time
51. Do
52. Meditation

ACKNOWLEDGMENTS

I would like to say that none of this would have been possible without your love and support. Thank you for believing in me and always giving me the encouragement to pursue my dreams..

CHALLENGING
OURSELVES
UNDER
REAL
ADVERSITY
GAINING
EMPOWERMENT

ENGAGE
FULL
FORCE
ON
REACHING
TARGET

Get
Our
Activities
Lined-up
Straight

Adjusting
Thought
To
Intentionally
Take
Us
Direction
Excellence

Find
An
Internal
Trusting
Home

URGES

- **U**NSTOPPABLE
- **R**ESPONSES
- **G**REATLY
- **E**NDANGERING
- **S**OBRIETY

FINALLY

EXAMINE

EMOTIONAL

LOSSES

G ENERATE
I NCREDIBLY
V ALUABLE
E XPERIENCES

GRADUALLY

RECOGNIZE

OUR

WAY

Lacking
A
Timely
Entrance

Let
Our
Vulnerabilities
Exist

MISTAKE

Making
Incremental
Steps
Toward
Achieving
Key
Efforts

MIXING

UNIVERSAL

SOUNDS

INVOKING

CREATIVITY

Opening

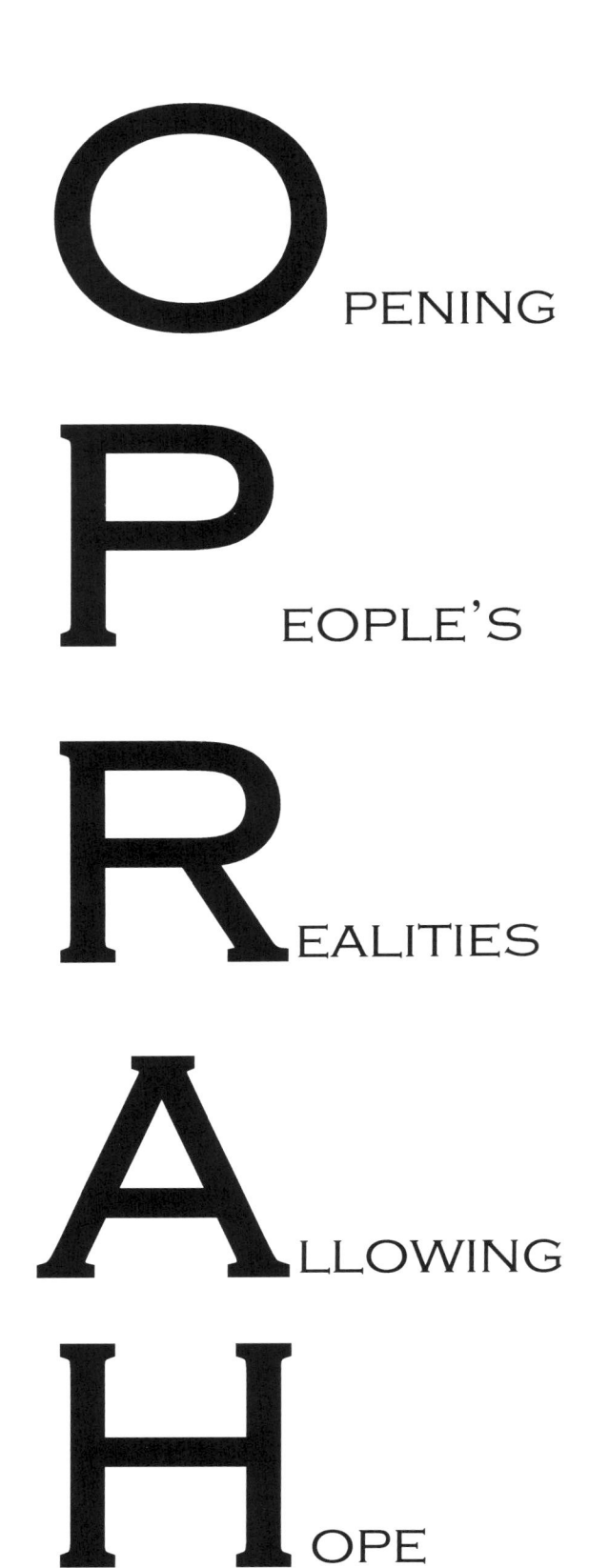

People's

Realities

Allowing

Hope

PURPOSELY

REPEAT

ACTIVITIES

CRITICAL

TO

IMPROVING

CORE

ELEMENTS

PUTTING

RESPONSIBILITIES

IN

ORDER

REGARDING

IMPORTANCE

TO

YOU

SLOWLY

ACCUMULATE

VALUE

EVERYDAY

Regaining

Every

Characteristic

Of

Value

Empowering

Real

You!

STRONG

EMOTIONAL

RELIEF

EXPERIENCED

NOW

INSTANTLY

TRANSFORMING

YOU

STRONGLY

HELD

ASSUMPTIONS

MINIMIZING

EXISTENCE

STRONG

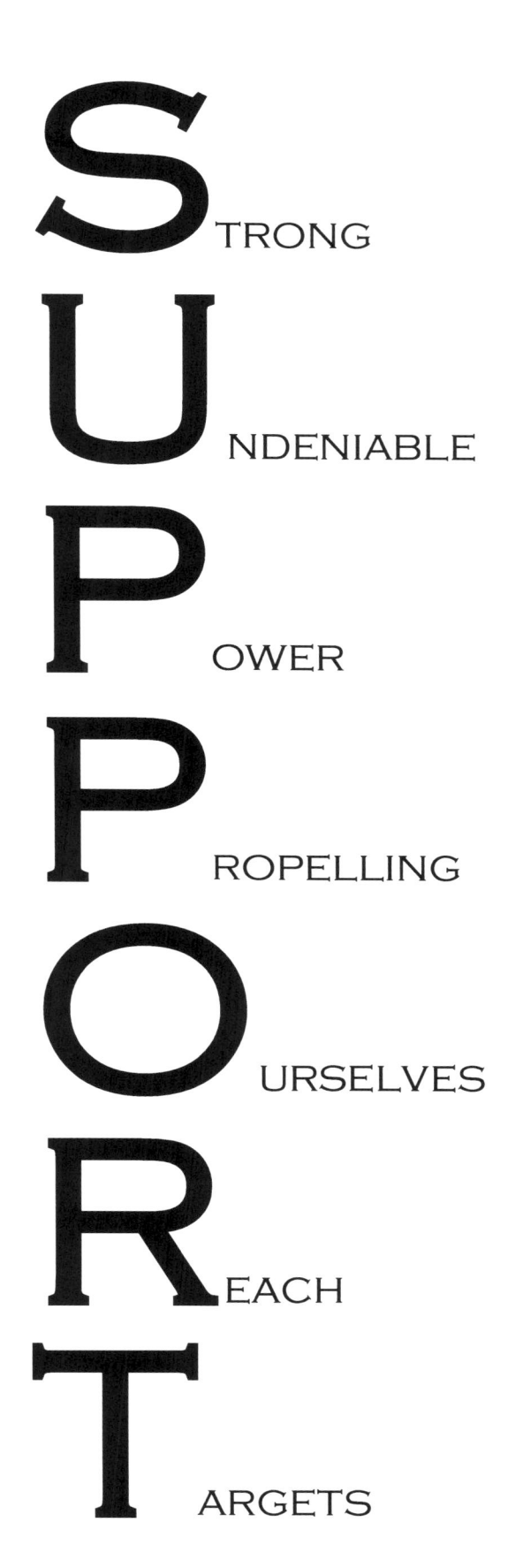

UNDENIABLE

POWER

PROPELLING

OURSELVES

REACH

TARGETS

The
Only
Day
Afforded
You!

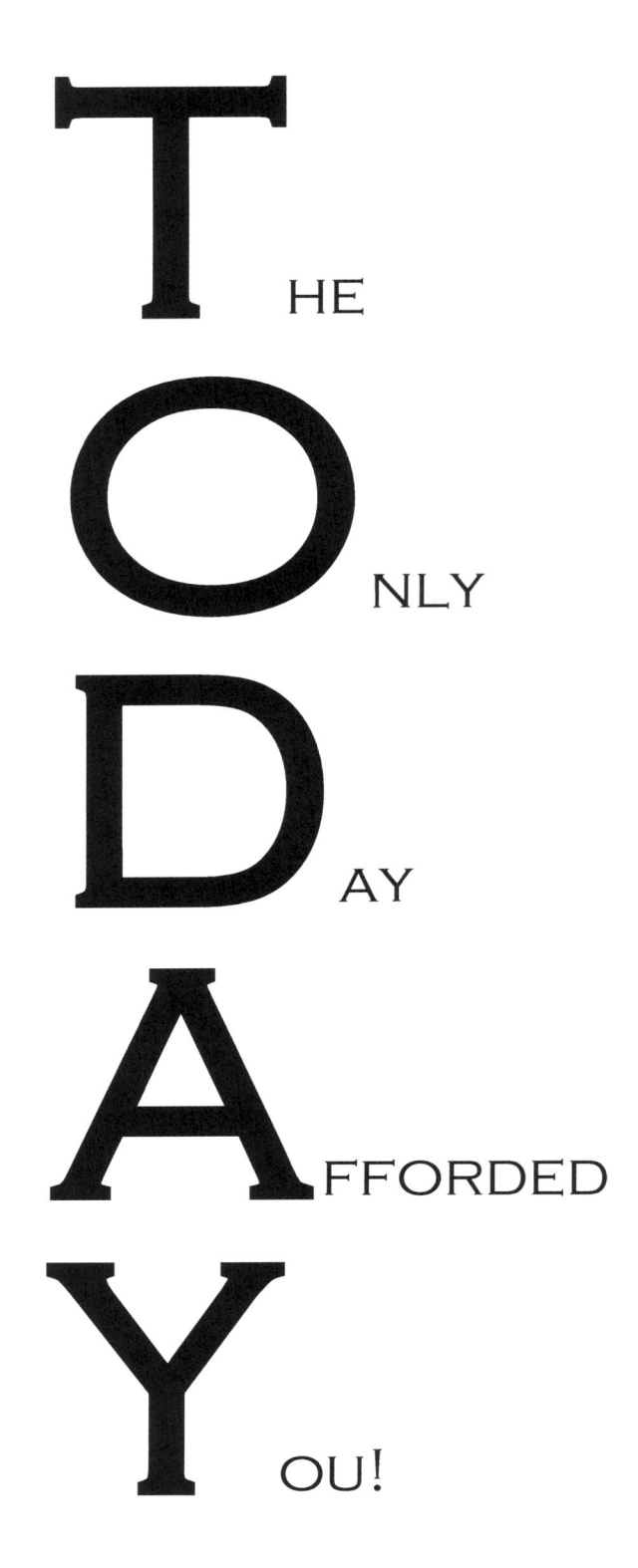

To

Risk

Uncertainty

Seeking

Togetherness

Waste
Hours
Analyzing
Things
In
Future

Waste
Hours
Analyzing
Things
In
Future

Will
Hold
You
Stuck

F ACE
A N
A
I MPORTANT
L ESSON

RE-EXAMINE

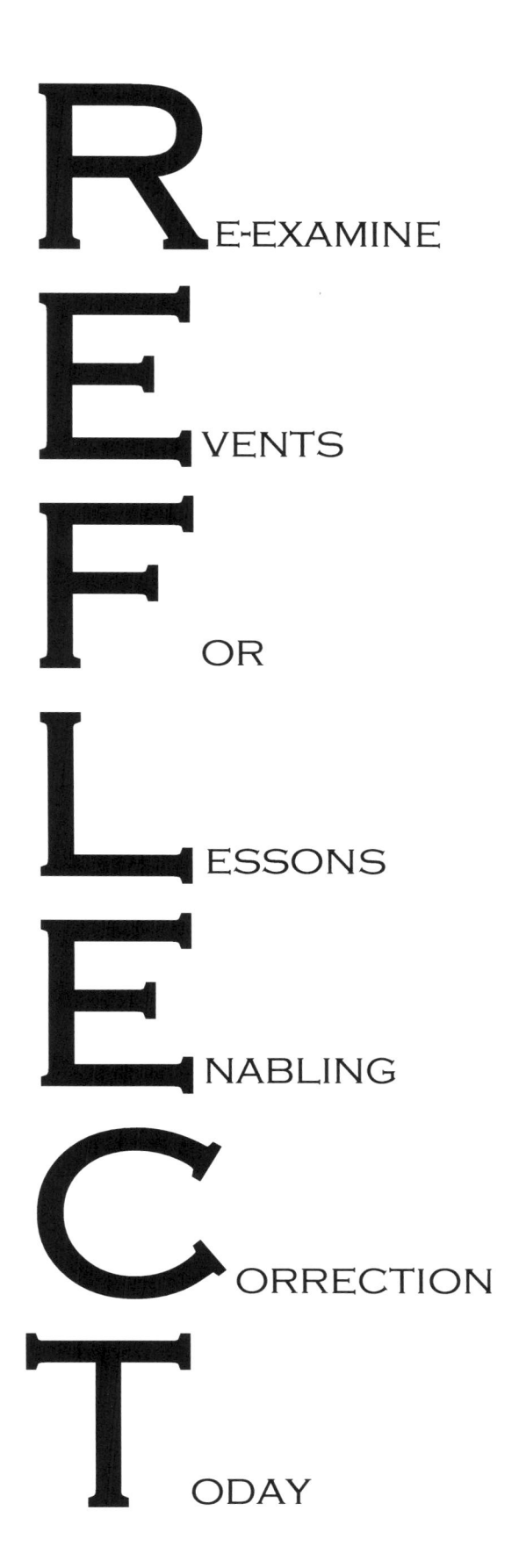

EVENTS

FOR

LESSONS

ENABLING

CORRECTION

TODAY

Actively

Work

At

Recognizing

Existence

© 2013 WELL YOUNIVERSITY PUBLICATIONS – Licensing Available

THRU

EDUCATION

AND

COMMITMENT

HELP

EMPOWER

RESPONSIBLE

STUDENTS

NURTURE

UNCONDITIONALLY

RESULTING

SPECIAL

EXPERIENCES

SHARED

DOCTORS

DELIVER
OUTSTANDING
CARE
TO
OPTIMIZE &
RELIEVE
SYMPTOMS

LAWYERS

LEGAL

ADVICE

WHEN

YOU

EXPERIENCE

REAL

SETBACK

T ogether
E mbrace
A
M ission

ACCEPT

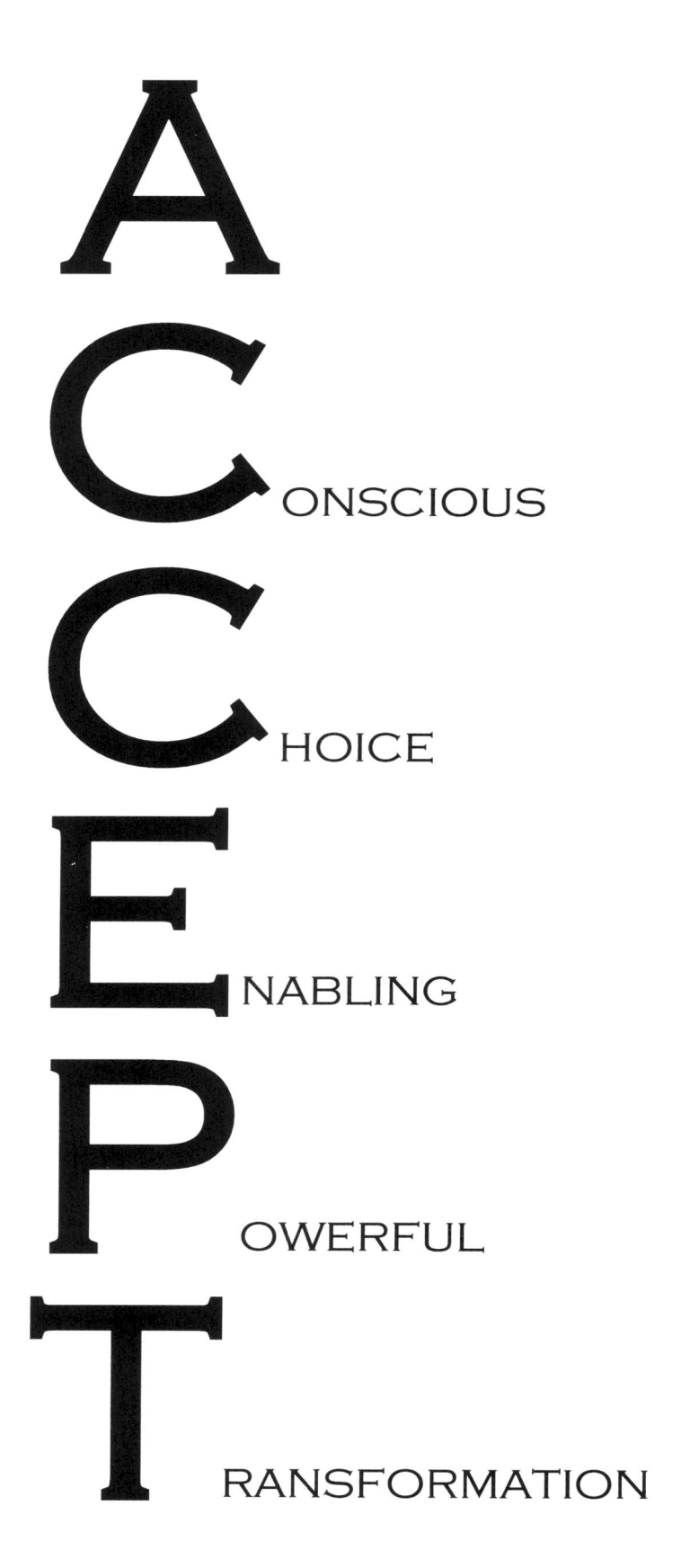

- **A**
- **C**onscious
- **C**hoice
- **E**nabling
- **P**owerful
- **T**ransformation

CLARITY

CLEARLY
LOOKING
AT
RESOURCES
IMPORTANT
TO
YOU

A

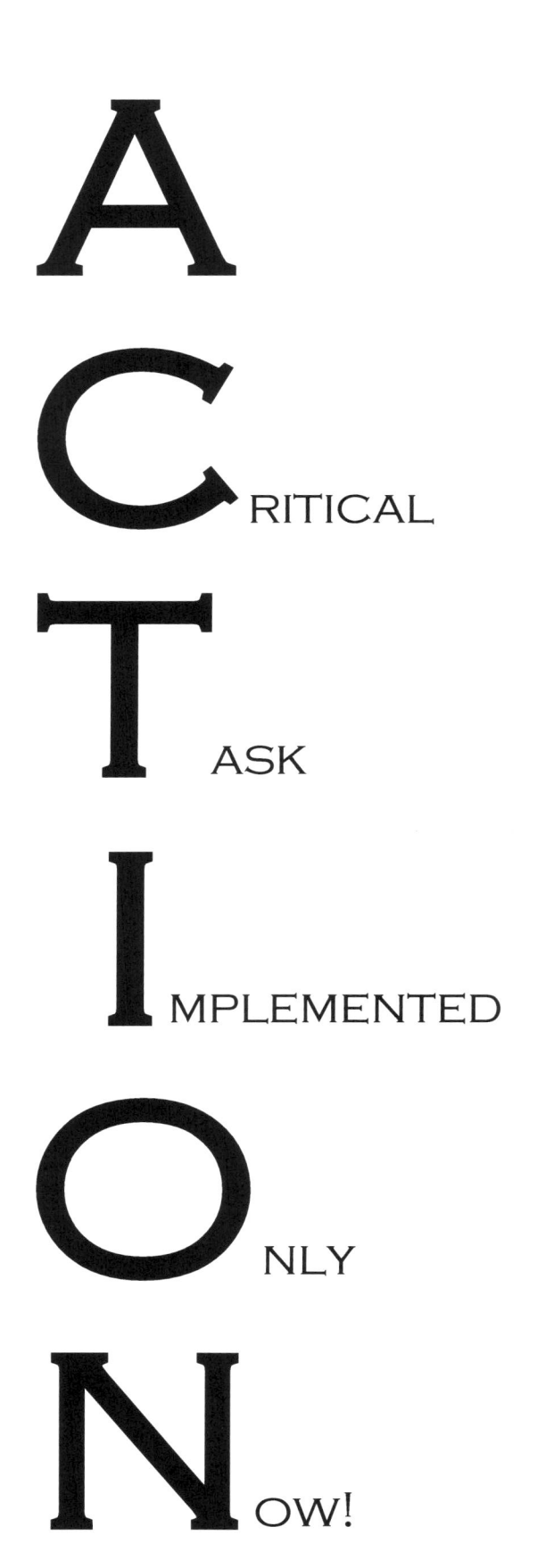

CRITICAL

TASK

IMPLEMENTED

ONLY

NOW!

GRIEVING

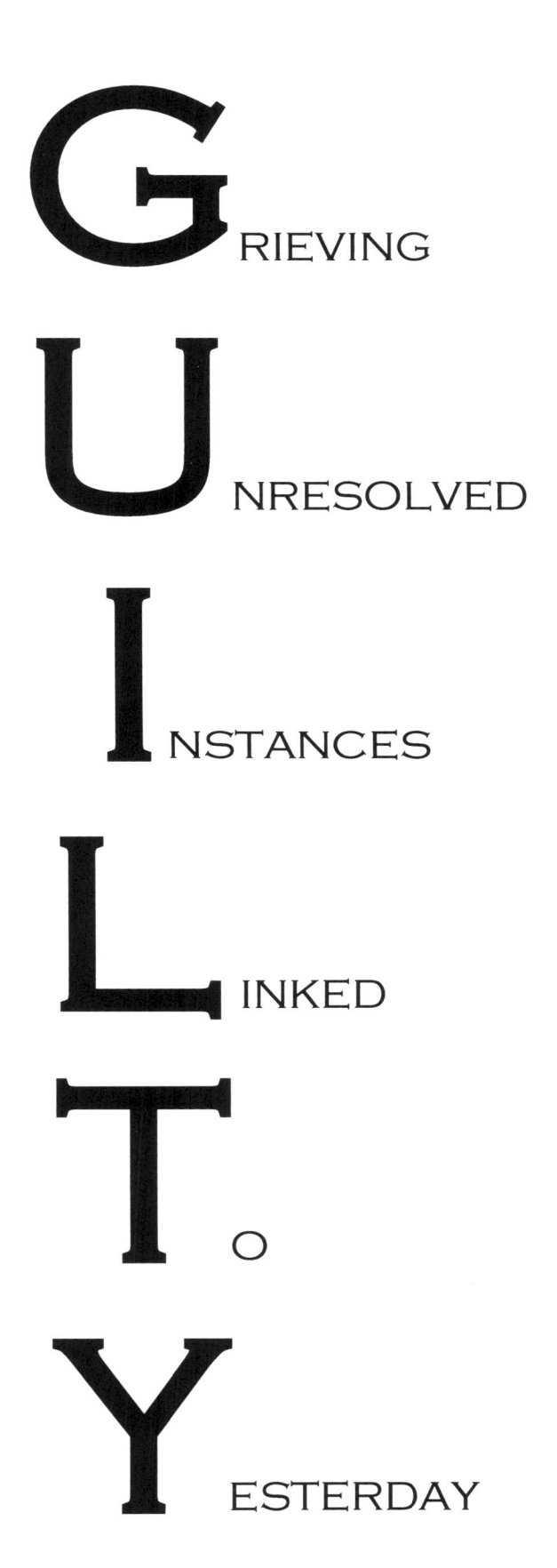

UNRESOLVED

INSTANCES

LINKED

TO

YESTERDAY

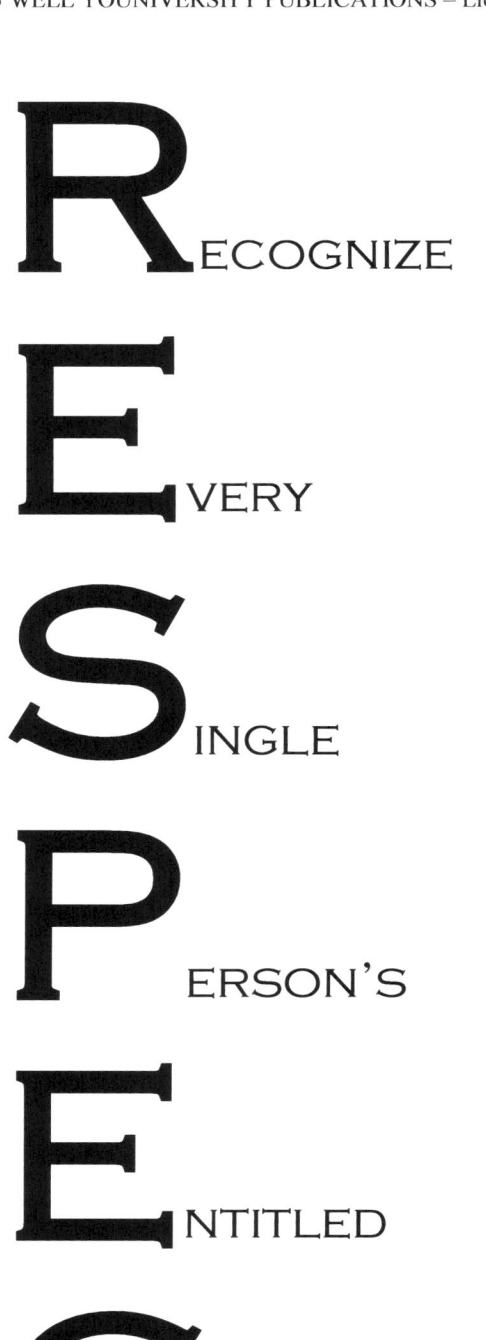

RECOGNIZE

EVERY

SINGLE

PERSON'S

ENTITLED

COURTEOUS

TREATMENT

BRINGING

OPPRESSED

NATIONS

OPPORTUNITIES

J UBILANCE
O VERWHELMS
Y ou!

Giving
Respect
And
Thanks
Everyday
For
Unbelievable
Life!

Swiftly
Take
Action
Reaching
Target

CHANNEL

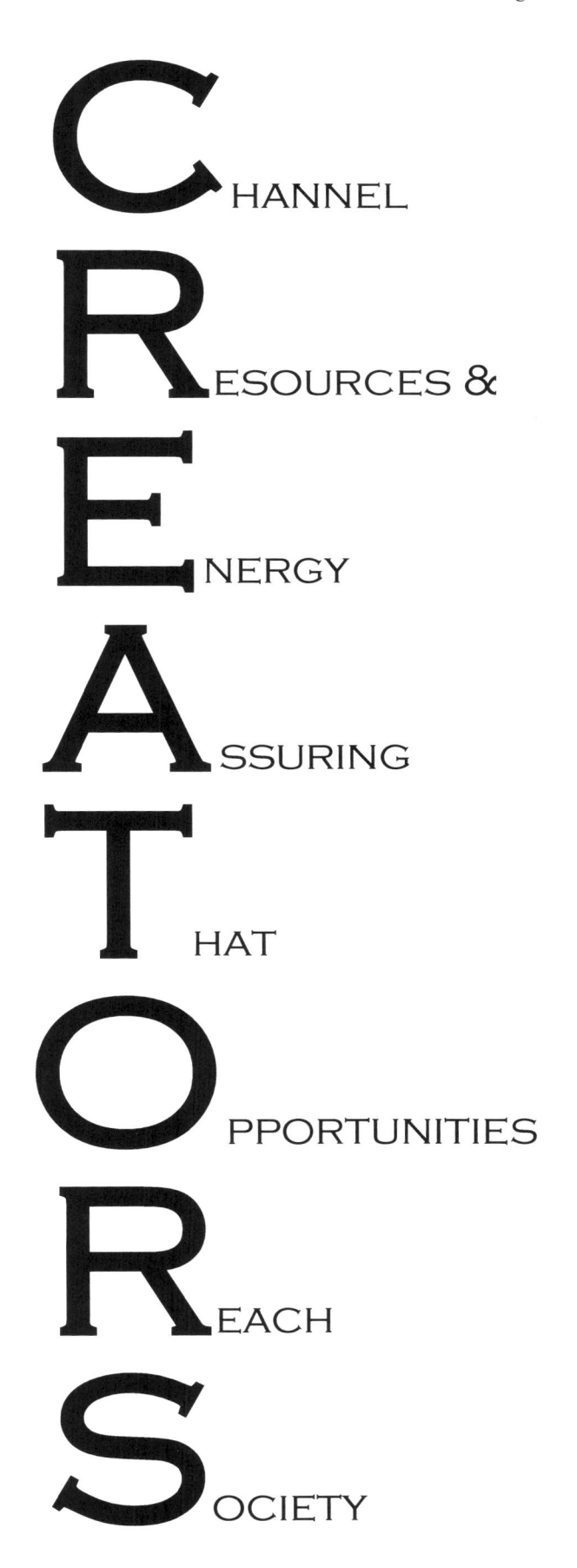

RESOURCES &

ENERGY

ASSURING

THAT

OPPORTUNITIES

REACH

SOCIETY

DEFINITELY

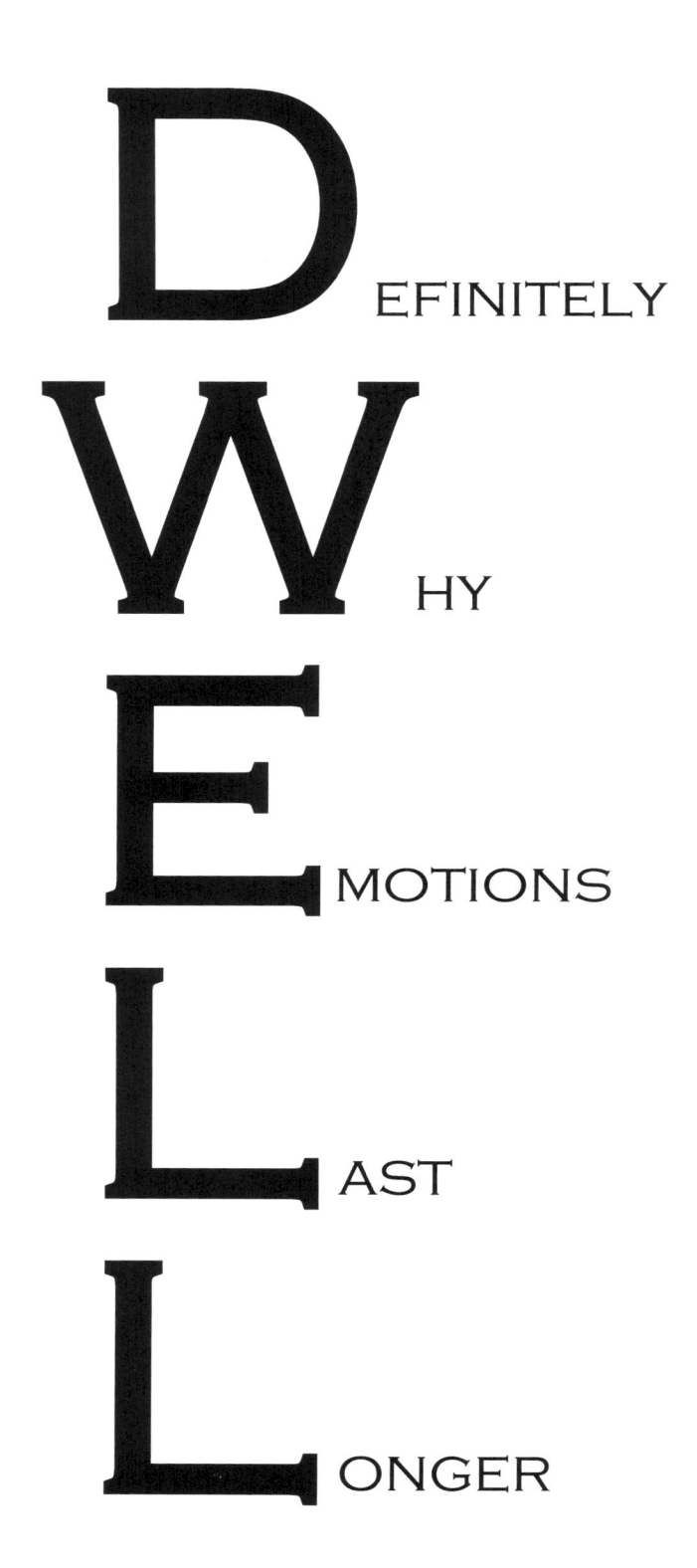

WHY

EMOTIONS

LAST

LONGER

Constantly

Having

Activity

Obstruct

Success

Find
Ourselves
Operating
Defensively

INTENSE

NEED

TO

EXPLAIN

RESPONSES

POSSIBLY

REACHING

EMPTY

TRUTHS

TRIGGER

The

Recognizable

Incident

Generating

Great

Emotional

Response

UNSTOPPABLE

RESPONSES

GREATLY

ENDANGERING

SELF

The
Instance
Marking
Existence

© 2013 WELL YOUNIVERSITY PUBLICATIONS – Licensing Available

Direct
Opportunity

MOMENTS

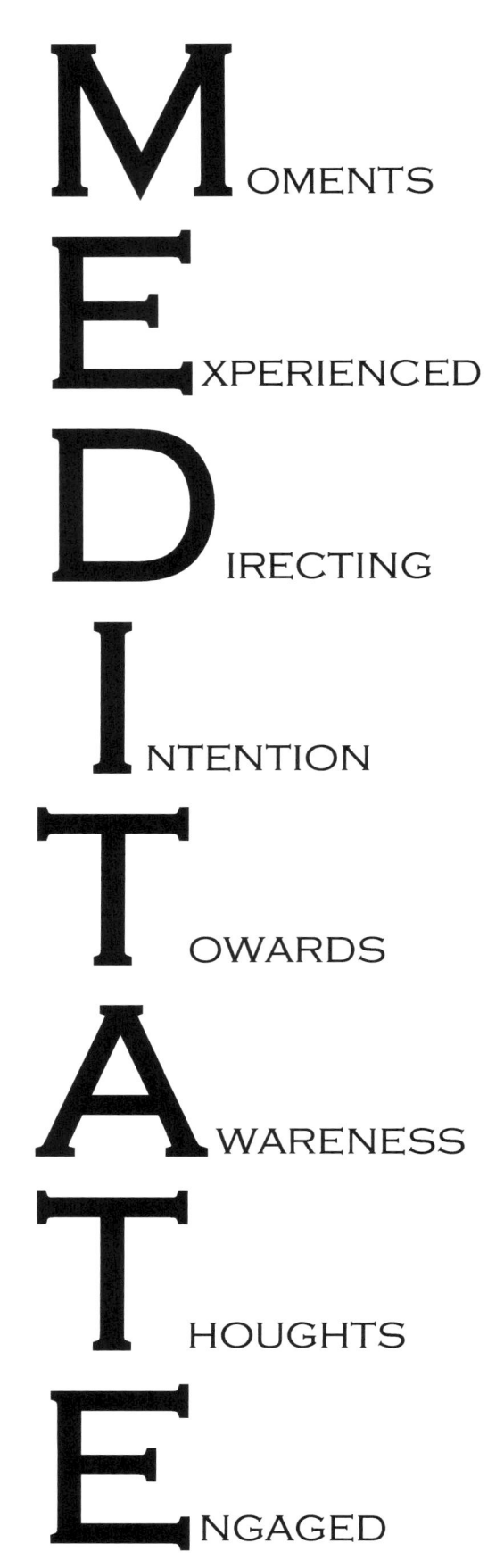

EXPERIENCED

DIRECTING

INTENTION

TOWARDS

AWARENESS

THOUGHTS

ENGAGED

ABOUT THE AUTHOR

Carol Rickard, LCSW, is a nationally recognized stress and wellness expert. She is the founder of Well YOUniversity, a health education company and author of several self health books including LifeTools, Putting Your Weight Loss on Auto, Emotional Eating, & Moving Beyond Depression. She is creator of the L.I.F.E. Recovery & Wellness Program, recently recognized by The Joint Commission (TJC)as a "leading practice". For information regarding wellness resources, training programs and workshops, please visit www.WellYOUniversity.com or email her at Carol@WellYOUniversity.com

OTHER BOOKS BY CAROL L. RICKARD, LCSW

Moving Beyond Depression: A Step by Step System for Reclaiming Your Life From Depression

Emotional Eating: How to STOP Using Food to Cope

LifeTools: How to Manage Life INSTEAD OF Life Managing You!

Putting Your Weight Loss on Auto: 7 Laws a Car Can Teach You About Lasting Weight Loss

Creating Compliance: A Toolbox of Coping Skills Handouts & Activities to Foster Treatment Compliance

Relapse Prevention: Reproducible Exercises for Relapse Prevention in Mental Health

Made in the USA
Middletown, DE
30 May 2016